T0314562

Don't
Waste Your
PUMPKIN

Don't Waste Your PUMPKIN

Emily Gussin

Innovative recipes and projects,
from *stalk* to *base*

murdoch books
London | Sydney

Contents

Introduction 6

Draw-o'-lantern 14

MAINS 20

Tablescaping 24

Pumpkin printing 32

Pumpkin wreath 38

Carving, but better 46

SNACKS & SIDES 58

Seed craft 62

Bird feeder 74

Peeled patterns 84

SWEETS 86

Place-card holders 94

Flower-pressed pumpkin 104

Index 108

Introduction

In the pages of this small book, I hope to bring you lots of inspiration. Pumpkin is one of those vegetables that, while fairly common, is a bit of an unsung hero.

For me, pumpkin forms the base of the season. Its association with autumn is iconic; its colours echoing the orange and green hues of falling leaves, and its sweet, nutty taste adding welcome warmth as the weather gets cooler. And of course, its association with Halloween is unrivalled. Unfortunately, as it's become synonymous with festivities we seem to have lost track of its best purpose: as food.

Food waste

In the UK, around 16 million pumpkins go to waste each year as they are carved for Halloween and then discarded. Our food system has a massive impact on climate change and food waste plays a huge role in that. When you also take into account the amount of people going hungry on our planet, it's deeply upsetting that we grow food simply to throw it away. I'm not here to lecture you, and if you've picked up this book, I assume that you already care about using your pumpkins; instead, I want to share practical advice for making the most of this brilliant vegetable. I've shared ideas for how to use pumpkins at Halloween without carving them, but also tips, if you do want to carve them, on how to go about it so they become more than just holiday decorations. And of course, this book includes lots of recipes that make the most of every part of the pumpkin, from the skin and the flesh to the pulp and seeds.

Versatile veg

As a recipe developer for a food magazine, my approach to writing has always been veg-first. Whatever dish I'm creating, I start by thinking about what fruits and vegetables are in season and then I build the other ingredients and flavours from there. So doing a deep-dive into one vegetable, be it one with many varieties, has been a treat. Pumpkin is incredibly versatile – the more recipes I developed for this book, the more ideas I had of how to use it. As pumpkins are in season during the bounty of autumn harvest, we are also spoilt with an abundance of fruit and veg at their best to enjoy with it. Plus they will last for months if kept untampered in a cool, dry place. My aim was to include something for everyone, to suit all tastes and occasions – and it proved easier than you would expect from a single-ingredient cookbook.

I think one of the best ways to combat food waste is to help people learn all the options available to use their ingredients. My recipes are simple at their core, the methods don't require exceptional skill and there aren't loads of ingredients. Instead, they show you how to build flavour and how to approach cooking with pumpkin. I've included exact measurements as expected, but I encourage you to taste and tweak as you cook. As someone who writes recipes for a living, I probably shouldn't admit that I never really follow them (outside of work). I read a lot of recipes and then riff off them based on what I have in the fridge and where my mood takes me. If you feel confident enough, I hope you use my recipes in the same way. Make the most of what you have: if you have onions instead of leeks, bay leaves instead of thyme sprigs, or white wine vinegar instead of lemon juice, that's fine. Cooking is more about flexibility and feeling than you may think. And if this suggestion fills you with dread, don't worry! The recipes are delicious if you follow them word for word (if I may say so myself).

Following the recipes

I've listed the amount of pumpkin you need for each recipe in weight, but do not worry if the one you choose is slightly larger or smaller than the weight required. In the case of the baking recipes, where a specific amount is more important, have a look through the book to use the rest of your pumpkin in another recipe. If you're unsure what you'd like to cook and your pumpkin needs eating, then I suggest making a big batch of the core recipes: the purée (page 16), stock (page 18) and seeds (page 60). You can keep the purée and stock in the fridge for a few days or freeze it to use later. Once dried in the oven, the seeds will last several weeks in an airtight container.

Pumpkin varieties

Having spent a good chunk of time cooking and eating pumpkin for this book, I urge you to source your pumpkins in the best way possible. Supermarkets are fine, but if you can support local farms and shops, you're likely to be rewarded by a bigger variety of pumpkins to choose from and a lot more flavour. As a general rule, the larger the pumpkin, the less intense the taste, but they do vary between the varieties. Here's a guide to the types of pumpkin you're likely to come across. In most cases, the only part of the pumpkin you can't eat is the stem. The skin may appear thick, but once roasted or cooked with the flesh, it becomes tender. The pulp and seeds require a bit more effort, but are easily prepared alongside another recipe. Anything you don't use can be composted, either at home or through a food-waste bin.

Jack-o'-lantern or carving pumpkin

This very large classic orange pumpkin is grown for size over flavour, but it is still edible.

Great for: purée (roast then cook in a pan to intensify the flavour).

Culinary or sugar pumpkin

This small to mid-sized classic orange pumpkin has more flavour than the larger carving varieties. It is subtly sweet and nutty.

Great for: purée, soups or stews.

Goosebump pumpkin

This pumpkin has wart-like bumpy skin, often with green patches. It is very similar to the culinary pumpkin, but its skin is too tough to eat.

Great for: purée, soups or stews.

Ghost or snowball pumpkin

This white variety has a very slightly sweeter flavour.

Great for: purée (roast then cook in a pan to intensify the flavour).

Crown Prince pumpkin

This pumpkin has blue-grey skin with orange flesh, a firm texture and nutty taste.

Great for: roasting in wedges or chunks.

Kabocha

This wide, flat variety has dark green or dark orange mottled skin and yellowy orange flesh, which is dense and nutty with lots of flavour.

Great for: roasting or frying in wedges or chunks.

Delica

This pumpkin has dark green skin with faint stripes. It has a flat shape and yellowy orange flesh. Its dense, sweet flesh has lots of flavour.

Great for: roasting or frying in wedges or chunks.

Munchkin

This small variety is flat in shape and its flesh is sweet in taste.

Great for: roasting.

Ghost Munchkin or Casperita or Baby Boo

Another very small variety with a subtle sweet taste.

Great for: roasting.

Pink porcelain or porcelain doll

This pale pink/orange-skinned pumpkin is fairly flat and thick-ribbed in shape. Its mid-density flesh has a sweet taste.

Great for: all rounder.

Musquée de Provence

This is a soft orange or soft green, large, flat variety with a thick-ribbed shape. Its mid-density flesh is sweet in taste.

Great for: all rounder.

Carnival or Harlequin

Small and ribbed with multicoloured skin, this variety is usually a mix of yellow, green and orange. It has a nutty flavour and strand-like texture.

Great for: roasting for purée or as wedges.

Project
Draw-o'-lantern

Drawing on your pumpkin is an easy way to get creative with your spooky decoration, without shortening its shelf life.

1. Felt-tip pens are great for drawing on pumpkins, or you can use edible ink pens if you plan to eat the skin of the pumpkin later.

2. Painting also works well. You can even get creative and use finger painting or handprints.

3. Draw a face for the classic Halloween look, or cover the pumpkin in a repeated mini ghost or bat pattern.

Pumpkin purée

There are two methods for making pumpkin purée; steaming is simpler, but roasting gives a richer, caramelised flavour. Either works with whatever amount of pumpkin you have.

For steamed pumpkin purée

Cut the peeled and deseeded pumpkin into 3-cm (1¼-inch) chunks. Pop them in a steamer or in a colander set over a pan of simmering water. Cover and steam for 20 minutes.

Check if it's tender with the point of a knife. If not, continue cooking for another 5–10 minutes.

Purée the pumpkin flesh with a hand blender or mash well with a potato masher. If the pumpkin is particularly wet, cook it out in a dry pan for 5–10 minutes over a medium heat.

For roasted pumpkin purée

Preheat the oven to 200°C (180°C fan/400°F/Gas 6).

Cut the deseeded pumpkin into quarters (unpeeled) and put the pumpkin on a roasting tray. Drizzle with oil, season with salt and roast for about 40 minutes until tender. Scoop the flesh from the skin and squeeze out the excess liquid.

Purée the pumpkin flesh with a hand blender or mash well with a potato masher. If the pumpkin is particularly wet, cook it out in a dry pan for 5–10 minutes over a medium heat.

Pumpkin stock

Make the most of every part of your pumpkin with this simple stock recipe, then use it to boost the taste of so many dishes.

scooped out pumpkin
  insides and seeds
pumpkin peel
other veg peel and
  trimmings (such as
  onion skins, carrot
  ends and peelings,
  cabbage cores, etc)
  or roughly chopped

celery, onion and
  carrot
herbs, such as thyme,
  parsley stems or
  bay leaves
a few peppercorns
large pinch of fine
  sea salt

Put all the ingredients in a large pan and cover with cold water. Bring to the boil then reduce the heat and simmer gently for 45 minutes. Strain the stock into a jug (pitcher) or container and discard the veg and herbs.

You can use the stock straight away, or allow it to cool and then chill for up to 1 week or freeze for up to 6 months. If you don't have lots of freezer space, boil the strained stock to reduce the liquid by three-quarters, then freeze in small portions. Reducing it will intensify the flavour to use like a stock cube.

If you don't want to make the stock straight away, store the pumpkin insides, seeds and skin, plus any other veg peelings and trimmings, in a container in the freezer until you're ready.

Mains

Pumpkin pasta

Whizzed pumpkin makes a silky coating for pasta in this easy weeknight dish. Top with a crunchy, seedy pangrattato topping for a no-waste dinner.

Serves 2

150g (5oz) dried
  spaghetti or linguine
1½ tbsp olive oil
2 garlic cloves, crushed
2 tbsp concentrated
  tomato purée
300g (10oz) Pumpkin
  Purée (page 16)
50g (1¾oz) full-fat
  cream cheese

20g (¾oz) Parmesan or
  vegetarian hard
  cheese, finely grated
40g (1½oz)
  breadcrumbs
1 tbsp Roasted Pumpkin
  Seeds (page 60),
  chopped
3 sprigs thyme, leaves
  stripped
salt and black pepper

Bring a large pan of salted water to the boil, then cook the spaghetti for 2 minutes less than the pack instructions, or until al dente.

Meanwhile, heat ½ tablespoon oil in a pan over a medium heat. Add the garlic, then, after a minute, stir in the tomato purée and cook for another minute. Spoon in the pumpkin purée, cream cheese and Parmesan and simmer for a few minutes.

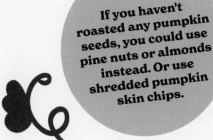

If you haven't roasted any pumpkin seeds, you could use pine nuts or almonds instead. Or use shredded pumpkin skin chips.

For the pangrattato, heat the remaining 1 tablespoon oil in a frying pan, then add the breadcrumbs and pumpkin seeds. Toast for about 6 minutes over a medium heat until golden all over. Season, then stir in the thyme leaves.

Once the pasta is al dente, drain it, reserving a mugful of the cooking water. Add the pasta to the pumpkin sauce and stir well until coated in the sauce. Splash in a little of the cooking water to help it combine.

Serve the pasta topped with the pangrattato.

Project
Tablescaping

The arrangement of decorative items and dinnerware has become the artform of the dinner party, and pumpkins are ideal as the centrepiece.

1. Start with the size and shape of your pumpkins – choose ones large enough to give a focal point to your table, but not so big they block conversation or get in the way. A few sizes and shapes will add variety and interest.

2. Think about your colour palette and textures. You could go for all orange tones, all white, greens and greys, or a mixture. If the pumpkins have a speckled appearance, try echoing this in your choice of napkins or plates.

3. Pumpkins can be the star of the table, but they will create more atmosphere if presented with other materials. Try foraging for long, loose trails of ivy or eucalyptus, or opt for dried flowers for a longer-lasting option. Candles also add mood.

Brothy beans with pumpkin

Comfort in a bowl, this simple dinner shines a light on the sweet warmth of pumpkin, pairing it with creamy beans and a seedy chilli oil.

Serves 2-3

3 tbsp olive oil

1 onion, sliced

1 tsp cumin seeds

2 garlic cloves, finely chopped

1 red chilli, finely chopped

1 tbsp Roasted Pumpkin Seeds (page 60), chopped

300ml (10fl oz) vegetable stock or Pumpkin Stock (page 18)

250g (9oz) pumpkin (unpeeled), cut into 2-cm (¾-inch) cubes

700-g (1½-lb) jar good-quality white beans, such as butter beans (lima beans), haricot beans (navy beans) or cannellini beans

100g (3½oz) cavolo nero, leaves shredded

salt

Heat 1 tablespoon oil in a saucepan. Sauté the onion over a medium-low heat with a pinch of salt and the cumin seeds for about 12 minutes until soft and light golden.

Recipe continues overleaf.

Meanwhile, make the chilli oil. Put the remaining
2 tablespoons oil in a small pan with the garlic,
chilli and pumpkin seeds. Cook over a low heat
for about 10 minutes to slowly release the
flavours without burning the garlic. Remove from
the heat and season with salt.

Once the onion is soft, add the stock and
pumpkin and simmer for 10 minutes. Tip in the
beans and their liquid and cook for 4 minutes.

Stir in the cavolo nero and cook for 1–2 minutes
until wilted. Season and serve topped with the
chilli oil.

Chickpea, pumpkin and coconut curry

Inspired by South Indian cooking, this vegan supper is tangy from tamarind, fragrant with curry leaves and has a hint of heat from the chilli powder. It is lovely served with rice or chapatis.

Serves 4

1 tbsp coconut oil
1 tsp black mustard seeds
12 curry leaves
1 onion, sliced
1 tsp ginger garlic paste
400g (14oz) pumpkin (unpeeled), cut into wedges 2cm (¾ inch) thick

400-g (14-oz) can coconut milk
2 x 400-g (14-oz) cans or a 700-g (24-oz) jar chickpeas (garbanzo beans), drained
2 tbsp tamarind paste
½–1 tsp chilli powder
½ tsp ground coriander
1 tsp ground cumin
½ tsp ground turmeric
salt

Heat the oil in a large pan, add the mustard seeds and, once sizzling, add the curry leaves. After 30 seconds, add the onion and cook over a medium heat for 8 minutes until softening.

Add the ginger garlic paste and cook for a minute, then stir in the pumpkin and cook for 5 minutes. Add the remaining ingredients and a pinch of salt. Simmer for 15–20 minutes until the pumpkin is tender and the sauce has thickened a little. Season to taste.

Roast pumpkin and carrot soup

Roasting the pumpkin and carrots before whizzing them into a creamy soup intensifies their honeyed taste.

Serves 4

800g (1¾lb) pumpkin (unpeeled unless the skin is very thick), cut into slices about 2cm (¾ inch) thick

200g (7oz) carrots, cut into rounds about 3cm (1¼ inch) thick

1 onion, quartered

2 tbsp olive oil

1½ tsp caraway seeds

150ml (5fl oz) double (heavy) cream

200ml (7fl oz) vegetable stock or Pumpkin Stock (page 18)

40g (1½oz) salted butter

20g (¾oz) Roasted Pumpkin Seeds (page 60)

salt and black pepper

Preheat the oven to 220°C (200°C fan/425°F/Gas 7).

Put the pumpkin, carrots and onion in a large roasting tray. Drizzle over the oil and season with salt. Scatter over 1 teaspoon caraway seeds and toss together.

Roast for 40 minutes, turning halfway through the cooking time, until golden and tender.

Crispy Pumpkin Skin Chips (page 64), shredded, also make a great topping for soup.

Scrape the contents of the tray into a blender and add the cream and stock. Whizz until smooth, then season to taste. Add more water if needed to get the right consistency, then transfer into a pan and heat through.

Melt the butter in a small frying pan until bubbling, then add the pumpkin seeds and remaining ½ teaspoon caraway seeds. Cook for a few minutes until nutty and toasted. Spoon on top of the soup to serve.

Mains

Project
Pumpkin printing

Potato printing is a great activity to do with kids, so why not try it with pumpkin?

1. Wash and dry your pumpkin, then cut it into shapes for printing. If you have small ones, you can simply cut them in half. If you have a large pumpkin that was previously used for carving, cut it into large chunks, then score a shape into the flesh – cookie cutters can help here.

2. Dab the pumpkin dry before applying paint with a brush, then press down to transfer the print to your paper or the canvas of your choice.

Sausage, pumpkin and apple traybake

Chucking everything on a tray and letting it roast is the easiest way to make dinner. Great served with mashed potatoes.

Serves 3

6 outdoor-bred pork
  sausages
500g (1lb 2oz) pumpkin
  (unpeeled), cut into
  wedges 2cm (¾ inch)
  thick
250g (9oz) beetroot
  (beets), cut into
  wedges 3cm (1¼
  inch) thick

1 onion, cut into wedges
  2cm (¾ inch) thick
1 apple, cored and cut
  into wedges 2cm
  (¾ inch) thick
3 sprigs rosemary
1 tbsp olive oil
200ml (7fl oz) dry cider
2 tbsp crème fraîche
100g (3½oz) kale, stems
  removed and leaves
  torn
salt and black pepper

Preheat the oven to 200°C (180°C fan/400°F/Gas 6).
Spread the sausages, pumpkin, beetroot, onion, apple and rosemary out on a large, deep baking tray. Drizzle with the oil and season with salt and pepper. Roast for 20 minutes.

Turn everything in the tray over and add the cider. Return to the oven for 15 minutes. Stir in the crème fraîche and add the kale, then roast for another 5 minutes before serving.

Pumpkin rösti

Perfect for brunch, in this recipe a combination of grated pumpkin, potato and onion gives an autumnal twist on classic hash browns. Serve them with fried or poached eggs and mushrooms.

Serves 2

200g (7oz) pumpkin
(unpeeled)
100g (3½oz) potato
(unpeeled)
1 small onion

1 egg
3 sage leaves, shredded,
or 1 tsp thyme leaves
½ tsp fine sea salt
2 tbsp olive or rapeseed
oil

Grate the pumpkin, potato and onion into a bowl, then put them in a tea towel and squeeze out the excess liquid.

Lightly beat the egg in a large bowl, then add the grated veg, herbs and salt. Stir together, then divide into six patties, shaping and pressing them together with your hands.

Heat a large frying pan over a medium heat and add the oil. Fry the rösti in batches for 3–4 minutes on each side until golden and crisp. Keep warm while you fry the rest.

Mushroom, leek and pumpkin turnovers

These quick pies are great for lunch or enjoyed with potato wedges and salad for dinner.

Serves 4

30g (1oz) unsalted butter
½ tsp caraway seeds
1 tsp nigella seeds
1 small leek, thinly sliced
200g (7oz) pumpkin, cut into 1-cm (½-inch) chunks
100g (3½oz) chestnut or button mushrooms, sliced
3 tbsp crème fraîche
1 free-range egg, beaten
320g (11oz) puff pastry sheet
salt and black pepper

Melt the butter in a pan over a medium heat. Add the caraway seeds, ½ teaspoon nigella seeds, the leek and a pinch of salt and sauté for 5 minutes until the leek is softening.

Add the pumpkin and cook for 5 minutes, then add the mushrooms and fry for 2–3 minutes over a medium-high heat to get a bit of colour.

Stir through the crème fraîche and half the beaten egg. Season to taste and scrape into a bowl. Set aside to cool.

Preheat the oven to 220°C (200°C fan/425°F/ Gas 7).

Unroll the pastry, cut it in half lengthways and then widthways to create four rectangles. Place them on a baking tray and divide the cooled pie filling evenly between the four sheets, placing it onto one side of each rectangle, leaving a 1-cm (½-inch) border.

Brush the border with beaten egg, then fold over the pastry to encase the filling. Use a fork to seal and crimp the edges, then brush the tops with more egg and scatter over the remaining ½ teaspoon nigella seeds.

Bake for about 20 minutes until golden.

Project
Pumpkin wreath

Displaying a wreath decorated with mini pumpkins on your door gives a glow of autumnal feeling for all to see.

1. Start with a metal wreath ring and some wire. Secure the end of the wire to the ring then wrap it around the frame, adding foliage as you gradually move around the ring and building up as you go.

2. The foliage is the base on which you can build your design. Use invisible wire or thin ribbon to strap mini pumpkins to the ring frame, tying them securely at the back.

3. You could also add flowers in similar colours to the pumpkins, ribbons or other decorations. Just be careful to not overload the frame and make it too heavy. Secure a ribbon or some twine to the top of the frame and use this to hang it on your door.

Pumpkin and burrata grain salad

A tangy pomegranate molasses dressing brings together sweet pumpkin, bitter chicory (witlof) leaves, fragrant dill, salty capers and creamy burrata in this hearty grain salad.

Serves 4-6

600g (1lb 5oz) pumpkin (unpeeled), cut into 3-cm (1¼-inch) chunks or wedges

5 tbsp extra virgin olive oil

30g (1oz) pistachios, roughly chopped

150g (5oz) pearl barley or freekeh

2 tbsp white wine vinegar

2 tbsp pomegranate molasses

2 tsp capers

20g (¾oz) dill, fronds chopped

2 chicory (witlof) heads, leaves separated

1 ball burrata

½ tsp pul biber or chilli flakes

salt and black pepper

Preheat the oven to 220°C (200°C fan/425°F/Gas 7).

Spread the pumpkin out on a baking tray, drizzle with 1 tablespoon oil and season. Roast for 30–35 minutes until tender and lightly caramelised.

Recipe continues overleaf.

Swap the pearl barley out for any grain you have. The recipe works well with wild rice or lentils too.

Toast the nuts on a separate tray for about 8 minutes.

Meanwhile, cook the grain of your choice according to the pack instructions.

In a jug, whisk the remaining 4 tablespoons olive oil with the vinegar and molasses, then season.

Add the warm grains, capers and dill to a bowl, then toss through most of the dressing, followed by the chicory.

Transfer the salad to a serving platter, scatter over the pumpkin and the nuts, then add the burrata on top. Drizzle with the remaining dressing and scatter over the pul biber.

Lentil-stuffed pumpkins

Tangy tomato and balsamic coated lentils are delicious with caramelised, roast pumpkin. I recommend Puy lentils here.

Serves 4

2 small pumpkins
2 tbsp olive oil
½ tsp fennel seeds, crushed
1 onion, sliced
150g (5oz) dried Puy or green lentils, rinsed

400-g (14-oz) can chopped tomatoes
2 garlic cloves, crushed
300ml (10fl oz) vegetable stock
20g (¾oz) parsley, finely chopped
1 tbsp balsamic vinegar
salt and black pepper

Preheat the oven to 200°C (180°C fan/400°F/Gas 6).

Cut the pumpkins in half and scoop out the seeds (reserve these for making Roasted Pumpkin Seeds on page 60). Place the pumpkin halves on a baking tray and drizzle with 1 tablespoon oil. Roast for 40–45 minutes until tender.

Meanwhile, heat the remaining oil in a saucepan. Add the fennel seeds, onion and a pinch of salt. Sauté for 8 minutes until golden and softened. Stir in the lentils, tomatoes, garlic and stock. Cover and simmer gently for 30–35 minutes until the lentils are tender.

Add the parsley and vinegar and season to taste, then cook for a few more minutes, uncovered. Spoon into the pumpkins to serve.

Pumpkin and goat's cheese risotto

Roasted pumpkin purée and soft goat's cheese makes this risotto extra creamy.

Serves 4

30g (1oz) salted butter
2 banana shallots, finely chopped
1 litre (1¾ pints) vegetable or chicken stock
4 garlic cloves, crushed
300g (10oz) risotto rice
200ml (7fl oz) dry white wine

400g (14oz) Pumpkin Purée (page 16; see tip)
125g (4oz) soft goat's cheese
1½ tbsp balsamic vinegar
30g (1oz) toasted pine nuts or Roasted Pumpkin Seeds (page 60)
salt and black pepper

Put the butter in a large pan over a medium heat. Once melted, add the shallots and cook gently for about 8 minutes until soft.

Meanwhile, put the stock in another pan and bring to a simmer. Reduce the heat to low and keep warm.

Add the garlic and risotto rice to the pan of shallots and cook for about 3 minutes until the rice looks translucent at the edges.

You can roast the pumpkin for the purée at the same time as making the risotto.

Pour in the wine and let it bubble until almost fully reduced. Add the warm stock, a few ladlefuls at a time, stirring regularly, until all absorbed and the rice is tender. Don't let the rice get dry at any point during this process; it'll take about 40 minutes.

Stir through the pumpkin purée and goat's cheese and season to taste.

Divide the risotto amongst four bowls and drizzle the balsamic vinegar on top. Finish with the pine nuts or pumpkin seeds.

Mains

Project
Carving, but better

If you're set on carving your pumpkins in the traditional way, keep these things in mind, so you can still eat the pumpkin afterwards.

1. Choose a fresher pumpkin by checking it's firm and the stem is green rather than grey and woody. Store the pumpkin in the fridge or in a cool, dry place before carving.

2. Wash your pumpkin with warm water to remove any dirt, then dry it well. Make sure any tools you use to carve it are clean too, sterilising anything that's not usually used for food in boiling water.

3. Remove the base or back of the pumpkin to scrape out the insides – keeping the stem intact will help it last longer. Make sure you remove all of the pulp and seeds (save these for stock, page 18) to keep moisture at bay.

4. Put your pumpkin in a window rather than outside. Choose a cool spot and use an LED candle rather than an open flame. Only leave it for a day or two, before rinsing and cooking.

Pumpkin-topped fish pie

Vibrant orange pumpkin mash updates the classic fish pie. Any firm white fish works well here, so look into what the most sustainable choice is at the moment.

Serves 4

500g (1lb 2oz) pumpkin flesh, peeled and cut into 3-cm (1¼-inch) chunks

500g (1lb 2oz) floury potatoes, peeled and cut into 3-cm (1¼-inch) chunks

40g (1½oz) unsalted butter

½ tbsp olive oil

2 leeks, thinly sliced

3 garlic cloves, sliced

1 tbsp plain (all-purpose) flour

1 tsp English or Dijon mustard

100ml (3½fl oz) white wine

200ml (7fl oz) double (heavy) cream

10g (⅓oz) chives, chopped

about 450g (1lb) sustainable skinless firm white fish fillets (such as coley, pollock, haddock and cod), cut into 3–4-cm (1¼–1½-inch) chunks

200g (7oz) frozen peas, defrosted

salt and black pepper

16 x 25-cm (6 x 10-inch) baking dish

Preheat the oven to 220°C (200°C fan/425°F/ Gas 7).

Put the pumpkin and potato chunks into a pan of salted water. Bring to the boil, then simmer for 20–25 minutes until tender. Drain well, then mash, adding 20g (¾oz) butter and salt and pepper to taste.

Meanwhile, heat the oil and the remaining 20g (¾oz) butter in a pan and cook the leeks with a pinch of salt for about 8 minutes until soft. Add the garlic and cook for another 2 minutes. Sprinkle in the flour and cook for 1 minute, then stir in the mustard and wine and bubble until reduced by half.

Add the cream and chives and cook for 2 minutes, then season and remove the pan from the heat.

Season the fish chunks and arrange in the baking dish. Add the leek sauce and the peas, and stir through the fish. Top with the pumpkin mash, using a fork to give a rough topping. Bake for 20–25 minutes until golden.

Pumpkin mac and cheese

Serve this dish in the middle of the table for an impressive centrepiece. Make sure you scoop the pumpkin flesh out with the saucy pasta filling to enjoy the whole thing.

Serves 4

1 pumpkin, about 1.2kg (2½lb)
3 tbsp olive oil
30g (1oz) unsalted butter
30g (1oz) plain (all-purpose) flour
1 tsp English mustard powder
¼ tsp paprika
500ml (16fl oz) milk

150g (5oz) mature cheddar, grated
50g (1¾oz) Comté or Gruyère, grated
300g (10oz) dried macaroni or spiral pasta
50g (1¾oz) chunky breadcrumbs
30g (1oz) Parmesan, grated
salt and black pepper

Preheat the oven to 220°C (200°C fan/425°F/Gas 7).

Cut the top quarter off the pumpkin and remove the seeds, then place the pumpkin on a baking tray.

Recipe continues overleaf.

Chop the removed top into 2-cm (¾-inch) chunks (remove the stalk but only peel if very thick skin) and spread out on another baking tray. Drizzle both trays with oil, season and bake for 20 minutes.

Meanwhile, melt the butter in a pan over a medium heat then add the flour, mustard powder and paprika, and cook for a few minutes, stirring it into a dry paste. Add the milk a little at a time, stirring well with each addition to make a smooth paste and, once all the milk is added, a smooth sauce. Bubble for a few minutes to thicken a little, then add the cheeses and stir to melt. Remove from the heat and season.

Cook the macaroni in a large pan of salted boiling water for 2 minutes less than the pack instructions, or until al dente. Drain, then stir through the cheese sauce. Add the pumpkin cubes to the mac and cheese and stir to combine.

Pour the mixture into the roast pumpkin. Scatter over the breadcrumbs and grated Parmesan. Bake for 20 minutes until golden and bubbling.

Pumpkin saffron rice

Fragrant saffron, zesty lemon and fresh-tasting dill make this easy dish special, and grating the pumpkin makes it quick to cook.

Serves 2 as a main or 4 as a side

2 tbsp olive oil
1 onion, sliced
pinch of saffron
500ml (16fl oz) vegetable stock
250g (9oz) basmati rice
4 garlic cloves, sliced
400-g (14-oz) can or
325-g (11-oz) jar chickpeas (garbanzo beans), drained
400g (14oz) pumpkin (unpeeled), grated
grated zest and fresh juice of 1 lemon
10g (⅓oz) dill
2 tbsp toasted flaked almonds
salt and black pepper

Heat the oil in a casserole dish over a medium heat, then add the onion and sauté for 8 minutes. Meanwhile, put the saffron into the stock to infuse. Rinse and drain the rice.

Stir the garlic into the onion and cook for a minute. Add the rice, cook for a minute, then add the saffron stock, chickpeas, pumpkin and lemon zest. Stir then cover. As soon as it comes to the boil, reduce the heat to low-medium and simmer gently for 9 minutes.

Remove from the heat, without removing the lid, and leave for 10 minutes to finish steaming. Stir through the lemon juice, dill and almonds, then season to taste.

Pumpkin, mushroom & mascarpone lasagne

Creamy pumpkin mascarpone purée is contrasted with chunky bites of earthy mushroom in this saucy vegetable lasagne.

Serves 6

750g (1lb 10oz) pumpkin

500g (1lb 2oz) spinach

50g (1¾oz) salted butter

50g (1¾oz) plain (all-purpose) flour

300ml (10fl oz) milk

1 tbsp olive oil

600g (1lb 5oz) chestnut mushrooms, quartered

3 garlic cloves, sliced

½ tsp smoked paprika

100ml (3½fl oz) white wine

250g (9oz) mascarpone

about 300g (10oz) lasagne sheets

50g (1¾oz) Parmesan or vegetarian hard cheese, grated

salt and black pepper

18 x 25-cm (7 x 10-inch) oven dish

Preheat the oven to 200°C (180°C fan/400°F/Gas 6).

Make pumpkin purée with the pumpkin using the roasting method on page 16.

Put the spinach in a colander over the sink. Pour over the boiling water from a kettle then leave to wilt and drain.

For the white sauce, melt the butter in a pan over a medium heat then add the flour and cook for a few minutes, stirring it into a dry paste. Add the milk gradually, stirring well with each addition, until you have a smooth paste, and eventually a smooth sauce. Once all the milk is added, add 150ml (5fl oz) water and continue to cook. Remove from the heat and season.

Heat a frying pan over a high heat with the oil. Add the mushrooms in batches and cook for a few minutes, stirring infrequently, until golden in places. Once they are all cooked, tip them all back into the pan and stir in the garlic and paprika. Add the wine, and bubble to reduce by half. Stir in half the mascarpone.

Squeeze the excess water out of the spinach, then roughly chop it. Stir it into the mushrooms and season.

Stir the remaining mascarpone into the pumpkin purée. Season and mix together well. To assemble, spread one-third of the pumpkin mixture on the base of the oven dish, then top with one-third of the mushroom mixture. Add a layer of lasagne sheets, then spread over one-third of the white sauce. Repeat until you've used up everything and have three layers.

Scatter the cheese over the top and bake for 30–40 minutes until golden on top.

Venison and pumpkin cobbler

A hearty, slow-cooked stew for cold Sundays, this cobbler is topped with herby scones (biscuits) for a cosy one-pot meal. Venison is an eco-friendly meat, but, if you prefer, you can make this with regeneratively farmed beef instead.

Serves 4

1 tbsp olive oil

500g (1lb 2oz) venison braising steak, cut into chunks

2 large red onions, cut into chunks

1 tbsp concentrated tomato purée

1 tbsp plain (all-purpose) flour

750ml (1¼ pints) red wine

2 bay leaves

8 thyme sprigs

8 garlic cloves, sliced

600g (1lb 5oz) pumpkin, cut into 3-cm (1¼-inch) chunks or wedges

150g (5oz) unsalted butter

400g (14oz) self-raising flour

4 tbsp chopped soft herbs

200ml (7fl oz) milk

salt

Preheat the oven to 170°C (150°C fan/325°F/Gas 3).

Put the oil in a large, lidded casserole over a high heat, add the venison and sear it on all sides for 5 minutes until golden all over. Use tongs to lift it out onto a plate.

Add the onions to the pan with a pinch of salt. Cook for about 5 minutes over a medium heat until lightly golden in places. Stir in the tomato purée and flour. Cook for 1 minute, then pour in the wine and 250ml (9fl oz) water. Add the bay, thyme and garlic. Return the meat to the pan with any juices on the plate and nestle in the pumpkin. Bring to a simmer, then cover with a lid and transfer to the oven for 2 hours.

When the time is almost up, make the cobbler topping. Rub the butter into the flour or whizz in a food processor, then add the soft herbs. Add the milk, a little at a time, until the mixture comes together into a rough, soft dough. Divide into eight portions and dot them over the casserole.

Increase the oven heat to 200°C (180°C fan/ 400°F/Gas 6) and cook the cobbler for about 40 minutes without the lid until the topping is golden.

Snacks
& sides

Roasted pumpkin seeds

Often scooped out and discarded, the seeds from your pumpkin are totally edible and worth saving.

seeds from 1 pumpkin

Preheat the oven to 180°C (160°C fan/350°F/Gas 4).

Remove the seeds from the pumpkin, dropping them straight into a bowl of water. Once you've got all of them, use your fingertips to rinse them well and remove any attached pulp. Put them in a small pan of water, bring to the boil and boil for 5 minutes. Drain, then pat dry with a clean tea towel.

Spread the seeds out on a baking tray and dry roast them for 10–12 minutes until crisp. Allow to cool and store in an airtight container for 2 months.

For a tasty snack or to sprinkle on a salad, soup or pasta, add oil, honey or maple syrup and/ or salt and spices and roast for 5 minutes more.

Project
Seed craft

*Let the seeds from inside your pumpkin spark your imagination!
This is a project children will love.*

1. Follow the steps on page 60 to wash and dry the seeds from within your pumpkin, then let the fun begin.

2. Paint the seeds, if you like, or stain them with natural ingredients like strongly brewed tea or turmeric.

3. Use the seeds to create patterns on craft paper, sticking them in place with glue. They make beautiful petals in flower pictures, can form the texture of larger shapes or be used for geometric patterns.

Pumpkin skin chips

If you can't keep the skin on the pumpkin for a recipe, skin chips are the answer. They're easy to make and are a great snack, especially with aioli for dipping.

1 bulb garlic
2–3 tbsp olive oil
1 pumpkin
ground spices of your
    choice, such as

ground cumin, chilli
    powder or paprika,
    to taste
3–4 tbsp mayonnaise
flaky salt

Preheat the oven to 200°C (180°C fan/400°F/Gas 6).

Cut the top off the garlic bulb to expose the cloves. Lightly coat with 2 teaspoons oil then wrap in foil. Prepare the pumpkin by slicing away the skin (don't be tempted to peel it; the peel will be too thin) and cutting it into 5–7-cm (2–3-inch) strips. Pop on a baking tray, drizzle over the remaining olive oil, then toss together to coat properly. Season with salt.

Put the pumpkin strips and foil-wrapped garlic in the oven and roast the pumpkin for 20–25 minutes until crisp and the garlic for 25–30 minutes until very tender.

As soon as they come out of the oven, toss the pumpkin skin chips in flaky salt and the spices of your choice.

Squeeze the roasted flesh out of the garlic bulb into a bowl. Add the mayonnaise and a pinch of salt. Serve the aioli with the pumpkin chips for dipping.

Pumpkin, feta and tahini dip

Salty feta and creamy, nutty sesame tahini enhance the warmth of roasted pumpkin in this addictive dip.

Serves 6–8 as a snack

200g (7oz) feta
50g (1¾oz) Greek yogurt
400g (14oz) Roasted Pumpkin Purée (page 16)
4 tbsp tahini

3 tbsp extra virgin olive oil, plus extra to drizzle
fresh juice of 1 lemon
1 tbsp ice-cold water
1 tbsp Roasted Pumpkin Seeds (page 60)
¼ tsp chilli flakes
salt and black pepper

Put the feta and yogurt in a food processor and whizz until smooth. Add the pumpkin purée and whizz again.

Stir 2 tablespoons tahini together with the olive oil and half the lemon juice, then drizzle this mixture into the pumpkin mixture with the motor running until incorporated. Season and scoop into a serving bowl.

Whisk together the remaining tahini, the remaining lemon juice and the ice-cold water. Drizzle this over the dip along with some extra olive oil, then sprinkle with the pumpkin seeds and chilli flakes, plus plenty of black pepper.

Pumpkin and cheddar scones

Cheesy scones, fresh from the oven, are one of my favourite afternoon treats. Adding pumpkin gives a subtle sweetness and a tender crumb.

Makes 8

250g (9oz) self-raising
flour, plus extra for
dusting
50g (1¾oz) salted
butter, cubed and
chilled
75g (2¾oz) mature
cheddar, grated

100g (3½oz) pumpkin
(unpeeled), grated
1 free-range egg, lightly
beaten
100ml (3½fl oz) milk,
plus extra for
brushing
salt and black pepper

Preheat the oven to 200°C (180°C fan/400°F/Gas 6).

Put the flour in a large bowl with a pinch of salt and plenty of black pepper. Rub in the butter until the mixture resembles breadcrumbs. Stir in the grated cheddar and pumpkin. Add the egg, followed by the milk, stirring into the mixture with a butter knife to bring it together into a dough.

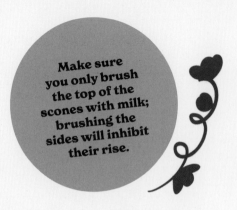

Make sure you only brush the top of the scones with milk; brushing the sides will inhibit their rise.

Tip the mixture out onto a lightly dusted work surface and knead as lightly as possible to shape it into a rough round. Pat or roll it out to about 2cm (¾ inch) thick, then use a 6-cm (2¼-inch) fluted cutter to cut into rounds. Push together the trimmings and repeat. Make a ball of any leftover bits to bake as a chef's treat.

Pop the scones on a baking tray and brush the top of the scones with milk. Bake for 14–17 minutes until golden.

Transfer to a wire rack to cool a little, then enjoy while still warm. These are best eaten on the day you make them, but will keep in an airtight container for another 2 days.

Snacks & sides

Loaded pumpkin fries

These nachos are loaded with black beans and given a pumpkin twist – they make a great sharing dinner or snack.

Serves 4–6

1kg (2¼lb) pumpkin (unpeeled)
2 tbsp olive oil
1 tsp ground cumin
½ tsp smoked paprika
2 tbsp Roasted Pumpkin Seeds (page 60)
1 tsp Tajin seasoning
200g (7oz) tomatoes, roughly chopped
1 small red onion, finely chopped

handful of coriander (cilantro), leaves picked and stems finely chopped
grated zest and fresh juice of 1 lime
4 tbsp soured cream
20g (¾oz) pickled jalapeños
400g (14-oz) can or 325g (11-oz) jar black beans, drained
100g (3½oz) cheddar, grated
salt and black pepper

Preheat the oven to 220°C (200°C fan/425°F/Gas 7).

Cut the pumpkin into 1-cm (½-inch) 'chips' (fries) and spread out on a large baking tray or two. Drizzle with most of the oil, season well and scatter over the cumin and paprika.

Recipe continues overleaf.

Roast for 35 minutes, turning halfway, until tender and golden.

On a small tray, toss the seeds in the remaining oil and the Tajin seasoning. Roast for 5 minutes.

Meanwhile, make the toppings. Stir together the tomatoes, onion, coriander stems and lime zest and juice, then season and set aside. In a small blender, whizz together the soured cream and jalapeños, then season and set aside.

Once the pumpkin chips are ready, pour the black beans over the top and cover with the grated cheese. Return to the oven for 5 minutes until melted and bubbling.

Dollop over the salsa and jalapeño soured cream. Sprinkle with the coriander leaves and the Tajin-spiced pumpkin seeds.

Snacks & sides

Pumpkin wedges with gremolata

Roasting simply in wedges is the best way to bring out the sweet, nutty flavour of pumpkin. A fresh and zesty gremolata sprinkled on top adds contrast and texture.

Serves 4 as a side

1kg (2¼lb) pumpkin (unpeeled), deseeded
2 tbsp olive oil
20g (¾oz) parsley, finely chopped (stems and leaves)
1 tbsp capers, finely chopped
grated zest and fresh juice of 1 lemon
salt and black pepper

Preheat the oven to 220°C (200°C fan/425°F/Gas 7).

Cut the pumpkin into wedges about 3cm (1¼ inches) thick. Coat with the oil, season and then spread out on a baking tray. Roast for about 30 minutes until tender and golden in places.

For the gremolata, mix the parsley, capers and lemon zest and juice, and season to taste. Spoon over the roasted pumpkin wedges to serve.

Project
Bird feeder

If you're going to carve a pumpkin for Halloween and leave it outside, it probably won't be edible for you, but it makes a delicious treat for your local birds.

1. When you carve the pumpkin, keep the scooped-out insides and seeds in a bowl in the fridge.

2. When Halloween is over, cut away some more of the top of the pumpkin to give a wider opening bowl shape. Scrape the pumpkin flesh with a fork to loosen it. Mix the reserved insides with bird-friendly seeds and fat, and pop this mixture inside the pumpkin.

3. Sit the pumpkin on top of a post or use twine to tie to a tree branch – choose a spot you can see from your windows, so you can enjoy watching the birds as they feast upon this autumnal treat.

Panko-crusted pumpkin

Crispy miso pumpkin slices make a great snack or starter, or you could serve them with noodles for dinner. Choose a pumpkin with dense flesh like Kabocha or Delica for this recipe.

Serves 2-4

400g (14oz) pumpkin
  (unpeeled)
1 tbsp miso
1 egg, beaten
3 tbsp plain (all-
  purpose) flour

80g (2¾oz) panko
  breadcrumbs
½ tbsp mirin
2 tbsp sake
2 tbsp soy sauce
2 tsp sesame oil
vegetable oil, for frying

Cut the pumpkin into slices about 1cm (½ inch) thick, and halve them if very long. Coat the pumpkin in the miso.

Put the beaten egg in a shallow bowl and spread the flour and panko out on two plates. Coat the pumpkin slices, one at a time, first in the flour, then the egg, then the panko, making sure you get an even coating.

Add enough vegetable oil to a frying pan to be 1cm (½ inch) deep and place it over a medium-high heat. Test the oil by dropping in a breadcrumb; it's ready when it sizzles within 15 seconds. Fry the coated pumpkin in batches for 2–3 minutes each side, until golden.

Stir together the mirin, the sake, soy and sesame oil. Serve the crispy pumpkin with the sauce for dipping.

Pumpkin, celeriac and potato gratin

Creamy gratins are the ultimate in comfort food. Serve this one with fish or chicken and a green salad.

Serves 6 as a side

600ml (1 pint) double (heavy) cream
400ml (14fl oz) milk
1 tbsp mustard
1 tsp fine sea salt
6 sage leaves, shredded
600g (1lb 5oz) pumpkin (unpeeled)

600g (1lb 5oz) celeriac (celery root), peeled
600g (1lb 5oz) floury potatoes
5 garlic cloves, sliced
80g (2¾oz) Comté, grated

30 x 20-cm (12 x 8-inch) baking dish

Preheat the oven to 190°C (170°C fan/375°F/Gas 5).

Put the cream, milk, mustard, salt and sage in a saucepan, bring to a simmer, then remove from the heat. Cover and set aside to infuse.

Use a mandoline or food processor to thinly slice the pumpkin, celeriac and potatoes. Layer half the vegetables in the baking dish, adding the garlic as you go, then scatter over half the cheese. Repeat with the remaining vegetables, then pour over the cream mixture. Top with the cheese. Cover with foil and bake for 30 minutes. Remove the foil and bake for another 30–40 minutes until tender to the point of a knife, golden and bubbling.

Cheesy pumpkin toasties

Meeting somewhere between croque monsieur and Welsh rarebit, this indulgent toastie will warm you up on cold days. Enjoy without the ham, if you prefer.

Serves 4

20g (¾oz) unsalted butter

20g (¾oz) plain (all-purpose) flour

1 tsp English mustard powder

½–1 tsp cayenne pepper, to taste

100ml (3½fl oz) milk

300g (10oz) Pumpkin Purée (page 16)

100g (3½oz) mature cheddar or Comté, grated

splash of Worcestershire sauce

8 slices bread

4 slices outdoor-bred ham

250g (9oz) Camembert or Brie, sliced

salt and black pepper

Melt the butter in a pan over a medium heat, then add the flour, mustard powder and cayenne, and cook for a few minutes, stirring it to a dry paste. Add the milk gradually, stirring well with each addition, until you have a smooth paste, then stir in the pumpkin purée.

Recipe continues overleaf.

Double the rarebit mixture and keep it in the fridge for up to 5 days to easily make another round of toasties.

Bring to a simmer and allow it to bubble for a few minutes, then stir in the cheddar to melt. Remove from the heat, season, and add the Worcestershire sauce.

Heat a grill (broiler) to medium-high and toast the bread on both sides. Spread half the cheesy pumpkin mixture onto four slices of the toast. Divide the ham and Camembert between the four slices and then top each with a second slice of toast. Coat the top with the remaining sauce.

Pop back under the grill for 1–2 minutes until golden, bubbling and melted.

Pumpkin, fig and apple chutney

Preserving is a great autumnal activity, filling your house with sweet, spiced aromas. It also makes the most of in-season pumpkin and apples to enjoy throughout the year ahead.

Makes 1.5 litres (2⅔ pints)

1kg (2¼lb) pumpkin (unpeeled), cut into 2-cm (¾-inch) chunks
500g (1lb 2oz) apples (about 4), cut into 2-cm (¾-inch) chunks
500g (1lb 2oz) onions, finely chopped

200g (7oz) dried figs, quartered
½ tbsp salt
2 tsp ground ginger
1 tsp smoked paprika
300ml (10fl oz) cider vinegar
500g (1lb 2oz) demerara sugar

Put the pumpkin, apples, onions and figs in a large preserving pan over a medium heat with the salt, spices and half the vinegar. Cook, stirring every now and then, until the fruit and veg release their liquid. Reduce the heat to low and cook for 1 hour until everything is very soft.

Recipe continues overleaf.

Stir in the rest of the vinegar and the sugar.
Cook for 1½–2 hours until the chutney is really
soft and thick. It's ready when a wooden spoon
dragged across the base of the pan holds a
separated channel for a few seconds.

Decant into sterilised jars, cover with a wax
paper disc and seal with vinegar-proof lids. Store
at room temperature for at least 2 weeks before
eating. It will keep unopened for 1 year in a cool,
dark place, but once opened, store in the fridge
and eat within a month.

Pumpkin ketchup

Homemade ketchup with a pumpkin twist has bags of flavour and makes a great gift.

Makes about 2 litres (3½ pints)

2 onions, chopped
2 celery sticks, chopped
1.5kg (3¼lb) pumpkin, peeled and roughly chopped
2 tbsp concentrated tomato purée

2 garlic cloves, chopped
130ml (4½fl oz) red wine vinegar
½ tsp ground cloves
½ tsp ground coriander
50g (1¾oz) soft light brown sugar
salt and black pepper

Put all the ingredients except the sugar in a large saucepan with 200ml (7fl oz) water over a medium heat. Cook for about 1 hour, stirring occasionally, to a pulp.

Whizz in a blender until velvety smooth, then pass through a sieve (strainer) into a clean pan. Add the sugar, then bring to the boil. Reduce to a simmer and cook until reduced and thick, about 20 minutes.

Remove from the heat and season. Transfer to sterilised bottles or jars. Seal immediately and cool. Put the sealed jars in a large pan of water and bring to a simmer. Cook gently for 45 minutes, then leave to cool in the water – they'll last up to 6 months in a cool, dark place. Once open, eat within 2 weeks and keep in the fridge.

Snacks & sides

Project
Peeled patterns

Carved pumpkins won't last long, so if you'd like to eat yours later, try etching a pattern into the skin instead.

1. Use a peeler and a small sharp knife to remove just the skin from the outside of the pumpkin in the pattern of your choice. Revealing the flesh will give a striking two-tone colour effect.

2. Choose spooky Halloween patterns, a jack-o'-lantern face or a group of ghosts. For an autumnal decoration, try etching away the shapes of falling leaves.

3. If you find freehand shapes tricky, use cookie cutters as a guide. Press them into the skin to cut the outline of a shape, then use a peeler or knife to remove the skin within the outline.

Sweets

Overnight oats

A few minutes of prep in the evening and you have an easy, nutritious breakfast in the morning. Customise the toppings depending on your mood.

Serves 1

50g (1¾oz) rolled oats
100ml (3½fl oz) milk, oat drink or water, plus extra if needed
pinch of cinnamon
50g (1¾oz) pumpkin (unpeeled), finely grated

1 tbsp nut butter
1 tsp honey, plus extra if needed
1 tbsp yogurt (optional)
1 tsp Roasted Pumpkin Seeds (page 60), roughly chopped (optional)
salt

In a container or jar, put the oats, milk, cinnamon, pumpkin and a pinch of salt. Stir together, then add a lid and pop in the fridge overnight.

The next day, add a splash more milk or water, if needed to loosen, and leave to come to room temperature for 30 minutes (or longer if you're taking them on the go with you). You can also warm them in a microwave if you prefer.

Top with the nut butter, honey and yogurt. If you'd like to add seeds too, heat them through in a pan with a little more honey until sticky.

Pumpkin fritters

These freeform doughnuts are spooned into oil to cook so there's no proofing needed. Quick to make and coated in cinnamon sugar, this treat is best enjoyed warm.

Makes 20

250g (9oz) pumpkin
(unpeeled, unless the
skin is very thick),
finely grated
130g (4½oz) self-raising
flour
1 tsp vanilla extract
grated zest of 1 orange
1 free-range egg, lightly
beaten

60ml (2fl oz) whole milk
70g (2½oz) golden
caster (superfine)
sugar
1 tsp ground cinnamon
salt
sunflower oil, for deep
frying
caramel sauce, to serve

Squeeze out any excess water from the grated pumpkin in a tea towel. Put the flour, vanilla, orange zest, egg, milk, 20g (¾oz) sugar and a pinch of salt in a large bowl and mix to a smooth batter. Stir in the grated pumpkin.

Recipe continues overleaf.

On a large plate, combine the remaining sugar and cinnamon, and line another plate with kitchen paper. Pour the oil into a deep pan until it's just under half-full, then heat until the oil reaches about 170°C (340°F) on a sugar thermometer (or a piece of bread sizzles in 15 seconds).

Use two spoons to scoop up a heaped tablespoon of batter and carefully lower it into the hot oil (if the fritters are too big, they won't cook through properly). Cook for 2–3 minutes until deep golden, turning over with a slotted spoon halfway through. Scoop out onto the kitchen paper to drain. Repeat with the remaining batter.

While the fritters are still warm, roll them in the cinnamon sugar then serve with caramel sauce for dipping.

If you have any leftover pumpkin flesh, scrape it out and keep it in the fridge in a sealed container to use in another dish.

Double the recipe and use a large pumpkin to feed a crowd.

Pumpkin pie

I use dark brown sugar in this American classic to give a rich, caramelised taste to the pie.

Serves 8-10

500g (1lb 2oz) shortcrust pastry

300g (10oz) Pumpkin Purée (page 16)

120g (4oz) soft dark brown sugar

2 free-range eggs

1½ tsp cornflour (cornstarch)

1 tsp ground cinnamon

½ tsp ground ginger

¼ tsp ground cloves

¼ tsp grated nutmeg

150ml (5fl oz) double (heavy) cream

black pepper

23-cm (9-inch) pie or tart tin

baking beans

Preheat the oven to 200°C (180°C fan/400°F/Gas 6).

Roll out the pastry to 5mm (¼ inch) thick and use to line the pie or tart tin. Trim the excess, leaving a small overhang (reserve the trimmings). Crimp the overhang then prick the base with a fork. Line with scrunched baking paper and baking beans. Blind bake for 15 minutes.

Remove the beans and paper and bake for 5 minutes more until dry. Reduce the oven temperature to 180°C (160°C fan/350°F/Gas 4).

Use any excess pastry to cut out decorative shapes, like leaves.

For the filling, put all the remaining ingredients in a large bowl with a good pinch of black pepper and whisk until well combined. Pour the filling into the blind-baked pastry case; it should come about three-quarters of the way up the sides. Add the pastry shapes around the edge.

Bake for 50–55 minutes until the centre is almost set with a little wobble.

Allow to cool on a wire rack for at least 3 hours to set properly before serving.

Project
Place-card holders

Mini pumpkins are the perfect size to sit on your table as place-card holders when you have friends coming round.

1. Use a sharp knife to cut a horizontal slice down into the stem of your mini pumpkins, being careful to not go all the way through.

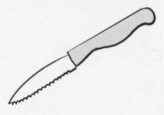

2. Cut some card into rectangles about 4 x 3cm (1½ x 1¼ inches) and write your guests' names on these. You could also illustrate these with little pumpkin pictures.

3. Add a little glamour by gilding the pumpkins with sheets or flecks of edible gold leaf.

Spiced pumpkin pancakes

The double treat: top these fluffy buttermilk pancakes with bacon and eggs for breakfast or with pecans and ice cream for dessert.

Serves 4-6

200g (7oz) self-raising
  flour
2 tbsp soft light brown
  sugar
½ tsp bicarbonate of
  soda (baking soda)
¼ tsp fine salt

2 tsp ground mixed
  spice
300g (10oz) buttermilk
200g (7oz) Pumpkin
  Purée (page 16)
2 free-range eggs
30g (1oz) unsalted
  butter, melted, plus
  extra to fry and serve
maple syrup, to serve

In a bowl, combine the flour, sugar, bicarbonate of soda, salt and spice. In another bowl, whisk together the buttermilk, pumpkin pureé, eggs and melted butter until well combined. Gently fold the two mixtures together using a rubber spatula, being careful not to overmix.

Heat a large frying pan over a medium heat and grease with butter. Once hot, use an ice cream scoop or a small ladle to add dollops of pancake batter to the pan, leaving space for the pancakes to spread. Cook for 2–3 minutes until they have started setting at the edges and bubbles are rising up through the batter. Flip and cook for 1 minute on the other side.

Keep warm on a plate covered with a tea towel while you repeat with the remaining batter. Serve with butter and maple syrup, plus toppings of your choice.

Leftover pancakes can be frozen in a freezer bag. Pop in the toaster from frozen to heat through.

Miso pumpkin cheesecake

Creamy and light, this Basque-style cheesecake is enriched with nutty pumpkin purée and umami-rich miso for a seductively sophisticated dessert.

Serves 10

600g (1lb 5oz) full-fat cream cheese
200g (7oz) golden caster (superfine) sugar
425g (15oz) Pumpkin Purée (page 16)
3 tbsp maple syrup
2 tbsp white miso

300ml (10fl oz) double (heavy) cream
3 tbsp plain (all-purpose) flour
2 tbsp cornflour (cornstarch)
5 free-range eggs

23-cm (9-inch) springform cake tin

Preheat the oven to 220°C (200°C fan/425°F/Gas 7) and line the cake tin with a large sheet of baking paper – it will be pleated and crumpled.

Recipe continues overleaf.

Put the cream cheese and sugar in the bowl of a stand mixer fitted with the paddle attachment (or use a mixing bowl and hand-held electric whisk), and beat on low speed for 2 minutes until smooth. Mix in the pumpkin purée. Mix the maple syrup and miso together, then stir this into the mixture.

In a separate bowl, gradually mix the cream into the flours with a rubber spatula to keep it smooth. Once combined, fold this into the main mixture on a slow speed. Add the eggs, one at a time, and mix until combined and silky.

Pour into the prepared cake tin and bake for 50–55 minutes until the cheesecake has a burnished tan colour on top and a good jiggle in the centre.

Leave to cool completely in the tin (it will drop in the centre – don't panic!), then cover and chill it overnight.

Bring to room temperature for 1 hour before unwrapping to serve. It will keep, chilled, for 3 more days.

Pumpkin spice cake

If you like carrot cake, you're going to love this pumpkin spice cake. Rich with cinnamon, ginger, cloves and nutmeg, dotted with pecans and drizzled with maple syrup, it's a crowd-pleaser.

Serves 12

220g (8oz) sunflower oil

4 free-range eggs

200g (7oz) soft light brown sugar

50g (1¾oz) maple syrup

275g (9¾oz) pumpkin (unpeeled), grated

300g (10oz) self-raising flour

1 tsp ground cinnamon

1 tsp ground ginger

½ tsp grated nutmeg

½ tsp ground cloves

75g (2¾oz) pecans, chopped, plus extra to decorate

salt

2 tbsp maple syrup

Cream cheese frosting:

120g (4oz) unsalted butter, softened

240g (8½oz) full-fat cream cheese, chilled

550g (1¼lb) icing (confectioners') sugar

½ tsp ground cinnamon

¼ tsp ground cloves

2 x 20-cm (8-inch) cake tins, lined

Recipe continues overleaf.

Preheat the oven to 180°C (160°C fan/350°F/Gas 4).

In a large bowl, mix together the oil, eggs, sugar, maple syrup and grated pumpkin. Add the flour, spices, pecans and a pinch of salt, and fold through.

Divide the mixture between the lined cake tins and bake in the centre of the oven for about 25 minutes until springy to touch. Turn out onto a wire rack to cool completely.

For the frosting, beat the butter with a hand-held electric whisk until soft and fluffy. Mix in the cream cheese until there are no lumps (don't overmix as it will become runny). Beat in the icing sugar and spices on a slow speed until just combined, then cover and chill until ready to use.

Use the icing to fill the cake and ice the top, then decorate with the extra pecans and drizzle the maple syrup over the top.

Project

Flower-pressed pumpkin

Pumpkins can become a canvas for flowers you have collected; simply use edible glue to paste them onto the vegetable's skin.

1. To make the glue, mix 200ml (7fl oz) water, 2 tablespoons caster sugar and 1 teaspoon white vinegar in a saucepan. Bring to the boil, stirring to dissolve the sugar. In a bowl, stir 2 tablespoons cornflour (cornstarch) into 150ml (5fl oz) water, then tip this into the pan. Boil for 2 minutes, then pour into a container to cool. Use within 1 month.

2. Make sure your flowers and leaves are clean, then arrange them on tea towels to dry.

3. Use a pastry brush to brush the pumpkin all over with the edible glue. Press your flowers onto the pumpkin, then brush with another light layer of the glue. Leave to dry.

4. When you're ready to eat your pumpkin, simply wash off the flowers with warm water.

Pumpkin and ginger loaf cake

With a craggy ginger crumble topping, this warming loaf cake is bound to become a regular bake as the weather gets colder.

Serves 10

220g (7¾oz) unsalted butter

225g (8oz) light brown soft sugar

2 free-range eggs

2 tbsp Greek yogurt

225g (8oz) white spelt or plain (all-purpose) flour, plus an extra 3 tbsp

1 tsp baking powder

½ tsp fine salt

½ tsp ground cinnamon

1 tsp ground ginger

400g (14oz) Pumpkin Purée (page 16)

50g (1¾oz) stem ginger in syrup, roughly chopped, plus 2 tbsp syrup

900-g (2-lb) loaf tin, lined

Preheat the oven to 180°C (160°C fan/350°F/Gas 4).

Put 200g (7oz) butter and the sugar in a mixing bowl and beat with a hand-held electric whisk to cream them together for a few minutes until light and fluffy. Beat in the eggs one at a time, followed by the yogurt. Stir in the flour, baking powder, salt, cinnamon and ginger, followed by the pumpkin purée and 1 tablespoon ginger syrup. Scrape into the lined loaf tin.

Melt the remaining 20g (¾oz) butter and stir in the stem ginger, 1 tablespoon of the syrup and the 3 tablespoons flour. Once clumping together, scrape the mixture on top of the cake in a craggy cover.

Bake for 1 hour 10 minutes–1 hour 20 minutes, until a skewer inserted into the centre comes out with only a few damp crumbs.

Allow to cool in the tin for 15 minutes, then lift out onto a wire rack to cool completely.

This cake freezes well if you don't need all of it in one go. Slice and separate with baking paper if you'd like to defrost a portion at a time.

INDEX

A

apples
  pumpkin, fig and apple chutney 81–2
  sausage, pumpkin and apple traybake 34

B

Baby Boo pumpkin 12
beans: brothy beans with pumpkin 27–8
bird feeder 74–5
black beans: loaded pumpkin fries 71–2
bread: cheesy pumpkin toasties 79–80
breadcrumbs
  panko-crusted pumpkin 76
  pumpkin pasta 22–3
brothy beans with pumpkin 27–8
burrata: pumpkin and burrata grain salad 41–2
buttermilk: spiced pumpkin pancakes 96–7

C

cakes
  pumpkin and ginger loaf cake 106–7
  pumpkin spice cake 101–2

capers: gremolata 73
Carnival pumpkin 13
carrots: roast pumpkin and carrot soup 30–1
carving pumpkins 10, 46–7
Casperita pumpkin 12
cavolo nero: brothy beans with pumpkin 27–8
celeriac: pumpkin, celeriac and potato gratin 77
cheese
  cheesy pumpkin toasties 79–80
  loaded pumpkin fries 71–2
  pumpkin and burrata grain salad 41–2
  pumpkin and cheddar scones 68–9
  pumpkin and goat's cheese risotto 44–5
  pumpkin, feta and tahini dip 66
  pumpkin mac and cheese 51–2
  pumpkin pasta 22–3
  see also mascarpone
cheesecake, miso pumpkin 99–100
chickpeas
  chickpea, pumpkin and coconut curry 29
  pumpkin saffron rice 53
chips, pumpkin skin 64

chutney, pumpkin, fig and apple 81–2

cobbler, venison and pumpkin 56–7

coconut milk: chickpea, pumpkin and coconut curry 29

cream: pumpkin, celeriac and potato gratin 77

cream cheese
miso pumpkin cheesecake 99–100
pumpkin pasta 22–3
pumpkin spice cake 101–2

Crown Prince pumpkin 11

culinary pumpkin 10

curry, chickpea, pumpkin and coconut 29

D

Delica pumpkin 12

dip, pumpkin, feta and tahini 66

draw-o'lantern 14–15

F

feta: pumpkin, feta and tahini dip 66

figs: pumpkin, fig and apple chutney 81–2

fish pie, pumpkin-topped 48–9

flower-pressed pumpkin 104–5

food waste 6–7

freekeh: pumpkin and burrata grain salad 41–2

fries, loaded pumpkin 71–2

fritters, pumpkin 89–90

G

Ghost Munchkin pumpkin 12

Ghost pumpkin 11

ginger: pumpkin and ginger loaf cake 106–7

goat's cheese: pumpkin and goat's cheese risotto 44–5

Goosebump pumpkin 10

grains: pumpkin and burrata grain salad 41–2

gratin, pumpkin, celeriac and potato 77

gremolata 73

H

ham: cheesy pumpkin toasties 79–80

harlequin pumpkin 13

J

Jack-o'lantern pumpkin 10

K

Kabocha pumpkin 11
kale: sausage, pumpkin and apple
    traybake 34
ketchup, pumpkin 83

L

lasagne, pumpkin, mushroom &
    mascarpone 54–5
leeks: mushroom, leek and pumpkin
    turnovers 36–7
lentil-stuffed pumpkins 43
loaded pumpkin fries 71–2

M

mac and cheese, pumpkin 51–2
mascarpone: pumpkin, mushroom &
    mascarpone lasagne 54–5
miso pumpkin cheesecake 99–100
Munchkin pumpkin 12
mushrooms
    mushroom, leek and pumpkin
        turnovers 36–7
    pumpkin, mushroom & mascarpone
        lasagne 54–5
Musquée de Provence pumpkin 13

O

overnight oats 88

P

pancakes, spiced pumpkin 96–7
panko-crusted pumpkin 76
parsley: gremolata 73
pasta
    pumpkin mac and cheese 51–2
    pumpkin, mushroom & mascarpone
lasagne 54–5
    pumpkin pasta 22–3
pearl barley: pumpkin and burrata grain
    salad 41–2
pies
    pumpkin pie 92–3
    pumpkin-topped fish pie 48–9
pink porcelain pumpkin 13
place-card holders 94–5
porcelain doll pumpkin 13
potatoes
    pumpkin, celeriac and potato gratin
        77
    pumpkin rösti 35
    pumpkin-topped fish pie 48–9
printing, pumpkin 32–3
puff pastry: mushroom, leek and
    pumpkin turnovers 36–7

pumpkin
    carving 46–7
    varieties 9, 10–13
pumpkin seeds
    roasted pumpkin seeds 60
    seed craft 62–3
purées
    roasted pumpkin purée 16
    steamed pumpkin purée 16

R
rice
    pumpkin and goat's cheese risotto 44–5
    pumpkin saffron rice 53
risotto, pumpkin and goat's cheese 44–5
rösti, pumpkin 35

S
saffron: pumpkin saffron rice 53
salad, pumpkin and burrata grain 41–2
sausage, pumpkin and apple traybake 34
scones, pumpkin and cheddar 68–9
seeds
    roasted pumpkin seeds 60
    seed craft 62–3

skin
    peeled patterns 84–5
    pumpkin skin chips 64
snowball pumpkin 11
soup, roast pumpkin and carrot 30–1
spiced pumpkin pancakes 96–7
spinach: pumpkin, mushroom & mascarpone lasagne 54–5
stock, pumpkin 18–19
Sugar pumpkin 10

T
tablescaping 24–5
tahini: pumpkin, feta and tahini dip 66
toasties, cheesy pumpkin 79–80
tomatoes
    lentil-stuffed pumpkins 43
    loaded pumpkin fries 71–2
traybake, sausage, pumpkin and apple 34
turnovers, mushroom, leek and pumpkin 36–7

V
venison and pumpkin cobbler 56–7

W
wedges, pumpkin 73
wreaths, pumpkin 38–9

Published in 2024 by **Murdoch Books,**
an imprint of Allen & Unwin

Murdoch Books UK
Ormond House
26–27 Boswell Street
London WC1N 3JZ
Phone: +44 (0) 20 8785 5995
murdochbooks.co.uk
info@murdochbooks.co.uk

Murdoch Books Australia
Cammeraygal Country
83 Alexander Street
Crows Nest NSW 2065
Phone: +61 (0)2 8425 0100
murdochbooks.com.au
info@murdochbooks.com.au

For corporate orders and custom publishing,
contact our business development team at
salesenquiries@murdochbooks.com.au

Publisher: **Céline Hughes**
Copy-editor: **Kate Reeves-Brown**
Designer and Illustrator: **Maeve Bargman**
Photographer and Prop Stylist: **Melissa
Reynolds-James**
Food Stylist: **Emily Gussin**
Production Director, Australia: **Lou Playfair**
Production Director, UK: **Niccolò De
Bianchi**

Text and design © Murdoch Books 2024
Photography © Melissa Reynolds-James 2024
The moral right of the author has
been asserted.

Murdoch Books Australia acknowledges the
Traditional Owners of the Country on which
we live and work. We pay our respects to all
Aboriginal and Torres Strait Islander Elders,
past and present.

ISBN 978 1 761500350

A catalogue record for this book is available
from the British Library

 A catalogue record for this
book is available from the
National Library of Australia

Colour reproduction by Born Group,
London, UK
Printed by 1010 Printing International
Limited, China

TABLESPOON MEASURES: We have used
15 ml (3 teaspoon) tablespoon measures.

10 9 8 7 6 5 4 3 2 1

MIX
Paper | Supporting
responsible forestry
FSC® C016973

About the Author

Emily Gussin is a chef, food writer and stylist based in London. She started her career in the world of cake magazines before training as a chef, completing a Cordon Bleu diploma. She has been Deputy Food Editor of *Waitrose Food* magazine and now works for *delicious.* magazine where she develops recipes, commissions contributors, styles the food and creates social videos. She also heads up the sustainability content, helping readers make ethical food choices and cut down on waste. She co-runs a seasonal supper club called 10 Miles Club for which the ingredients are sourced within 10 miles of the venue.